꿈꾸는 길, 산티아고
Dreaming Camino, Santiago

꿈꾸는 길, 산티아고
Dreaming Camino, Santiago

54일간의 800km 사진여행

글·사진 김창현

눈빛

들어가며

'산티아고 길'을 꿈꾼 적이 있습니다. 오래전입니다. 그리고 세월이 많이 흘렀습니다. 나이, 체력, 의사소통의 한계, 공황장애, 코로나⋯. 여러 이유로 국내 여행에 만족했습니다. 그런데 뜻하지 않은 암 진단으로 상황이 바뀌었습니다. 위기는 기회라고 했던가요. 젊은 시절의 꿈을 다시 꾸게 된 것입니다. 가족들의 응원도 있었습니다.

항공권을 예매하고, 관련 책들을 읽다 보니 남들처럼 책 한 권 내보고 싶은 생각이 들었습니다. 그리고 사진 전시회도 꿈꾸게 되었습니다. 꿈꾸는 것은 자유이니까요.

순례길을 걷기 전에 제목부터 정했습니다.
'꿈꾸는 길, 산티아고'

꿈은 이루어집니다. 마음 가는 곳에 길이 있게 마련이지요. 2022년 봄, 프랑스 길 800km를 남들과 달리 49일 동안 천천히 여유롭게 다녔습니다. 순례길은 감사와 은혜가 넘치고, 행복한 꿈을 꾸는 길이었습니다. 걷는 동안 은혜롭고 아름다운 모습에 자주자주 눈물을 훔치곤 했습니다.

이런 느낌을 나누고자 명동성당 '갤러리 1898'에서 사진 전시회를 열었습니다. 휴대폰으로 찍은 사진으로 말입니다. 생각 외로 많은 분들이 호응해 주셨습니다. 일부러 멀리 미국에서, 대만에서, 지방에서 와 주셨습니다. 같은 길을 걸었다는 이유만으로 말입니다. 여러 후원도 있었습니다. 적지 않은 수익금이 생겨 순례길 도네이션 알베르게 네 곳에 기부도 했습니다. 정말 감사한 일입니다.

그리고 이제 포토에세이를 준비하게 되었습니다. 사진에 담긴 당시의 단상을 떠올리면서요. 책 편집과 구성도 유튜브 영상으로 배우면서 직접 해 보았습니다. 제 사진의 느낌을 저만큼 아는 사람은 없을 테니까요.

순례길에서 수많은 외국 친구들을 만나고 그들의 사진을 찍었습니다. 지금도 연락하는 사람들이 있습니다. 이들 한두 명을 위해서라도 영문 설명이 있었으면 좋겠다는 생각입니다. 순례길에서처럼 번역기를 돌려 영문 번역을 하였고, 아들과 며느리가 날것과 다름없는 영문을 다듬어 주었습니다. 딸과 사위는 오탈자와 거친 문장을 바로잡았습니다. 이 책은 암을 통해 저와 가족에게 주신 하나님의 선물입니다.

산티아고 순례길을 걷는 사람들이 공통적으로 경험하는 것이 있습니다. 도움을 주는 천사를 자주 만난다는 것입니다. 저도 순례길에서 여러 번 천사를 만났습니다. 다녀와서도 마찬가지였습니다. 명동성당의 사진 전시회도 천사가 예비한 선물이라고 생각합니다. 한 해 대관이 다 끝난 시점에 신기하게 한 자리가 남아 있었습니다.

이 책도 마찬가지입니다. 눈빛출판사에 보낸 원고를 생면부지의 이규상 대표님께서 읽어 보시고 흔쾌히 출간을 허락해 주셨습니다. 부족한 사진과 글이지만 아담하게 세상에 빛을 보게 해주신 눈빛출판사에 깊이 머리 조아려 감사드립니다. 아울러 오래전의 인연으로 영문을 다듬어 준 홍성희 선생님께도 감사드립니다

'꿈꾸는 길, 산티아고'를 통해서 다녀온 사람에게는 영성이 넘치는 추억의 되새김 자리가, 아직 가 보지 못한 사람에게는 산티아고 순례길을 느끼는 자리가 되었으면 좋겠습니다. 한 가지 소망을 더한다면 산티아고 순례길에 이 책이 놓여 있기를 기대합니다. 계속 꿈꾸게 되는 산티아고 길입니다.

부엔 카미노 ~

2023년 봄날 김창현

Foreword

I once dreamed of 'Camino de Santiago.' It was a long time ago, and many years have passed since then. Age, physical strength, limitation of communication, panic disorder, corona... I had to be content with my domestic trips for many reasons. Then, unexpectedly, cancer changed the situation. Did someone say crisis is an opportunity? I was able to rekindle the dreams of my youth. There was also cheering from my family.

As I booked a flight ticket and read books about pilgrimage, I contemplated publishing a book myself. Then I dreamed of an exhibition. You are free to dream, after all.

I decided on the title before I left.
'Dreaming Camino, Santiago.'

Dreams come true. Where there's a heart, there's always a way. In spring 2022, I traveled 800km of the French route for 49 days. Unlike most others, I walked slowly and leisurely. The pilgrimage route was filled with gratitude, blessings, and happy dreams. While walking, I often wiped away tears at the grace and beauty I encountered.

To share this feeling, I held a photo exhibition at 'Gallery 1898' in Myeongdong Cathedral. The pictures had been taken with a mobile phone. Surprisingly, many people showed an interest in them. They came from the U.S., Taiwan, and rural parts of Korea for the exhibition just because we had walked the same path. I was able to raise quite a bit of money through the exhibition and donated it to four Donavito albergues. I am very grateful for that.

Now, I was ready to work on a photo essay. I retraced the impressions I had when taking each picture. I also taught myself book designing by watching YouTube videos. I wanted to do it myself because I knew no one understood what was inside the photos as well as I did.

I met plenty of foreign friends on the pilgrimage and took pictures of them. I still keep in touch with some of them. And I felt it would be nice to have English descriptions for them in the book. So, as I used to do on the route, I turned to an automatic translator to write an English draft. My son and daughter-in-law edited the very rough English words. My daughter and son-in-law also corrected typos and smoothed the sentences. This book is a gift from God to me and my family through cancer.

There is a common experience among those on the Santiago pilgrimage. It's that they frequently receive help from angels along the way. I also met angels many times on the Camino. It was the same when I came back. I feel the photo exhibition at Myeongdong Cathedral was also a gift from an angel. While reservations had been wrapped for the year, one spot was left open mysteriously.

The same goes for this book. Kyusang Lee of Noonbit Publishing Co., who had never met me, read the manuscript I sent and readily agreed to publish it. I am deeply grateful to Noonbit Publishing Co. for allowing my humble photographs and writings to see the light. I also want to express my heartfelt thanks to Sunghee Hong, whom I worked with many years ago, for polishing the English text.

I hope that *Dreaming Camino, Santiago* will bring remembrance to those who have gone on the pilgrimage and offer a glimpse of the profound journey for those who have yet to do so. To add one more wish, I hope this book will be placed somewhere on the Santiago pilgrimage route. Meanwhile, I go on dreaming about Camino Santiago.

Buen Camino ~

Changhyun Kim, on a spring day in 2023

'산티아고'는 예수님의 열두 제자 중 한 명인 '성 야고보'를 이르는 스페인식 이름이다. 그의 시신이 발견된 자리에 성당과 도시가 세워지고, 산티아고는 예루살렘과 로마와 더불어 세계 3대 성지가 되었다.

산티아고로 향하는 순례길은 여러 길이 있다. 이 가운데 가장 오래되고 보편적인 길이 프랑스 땅 생장피에드포르에서 출발하는 800km 여정의 '프랑스 길'이다.

'Santiago' is the Spanish name for 'Saint James', one of Jesus' twelve disciples. A cathedral and a city were built on the site where his body was found, and Santiago became one of the world's top three sacred places, next to Jerusalem and Rome.

There are many pilgrimage routes to Santiago. The oldest and most commonly taken road is 'The French Route', an 800km journey that begins at Saint-Jean-Pied-de-Port, France.

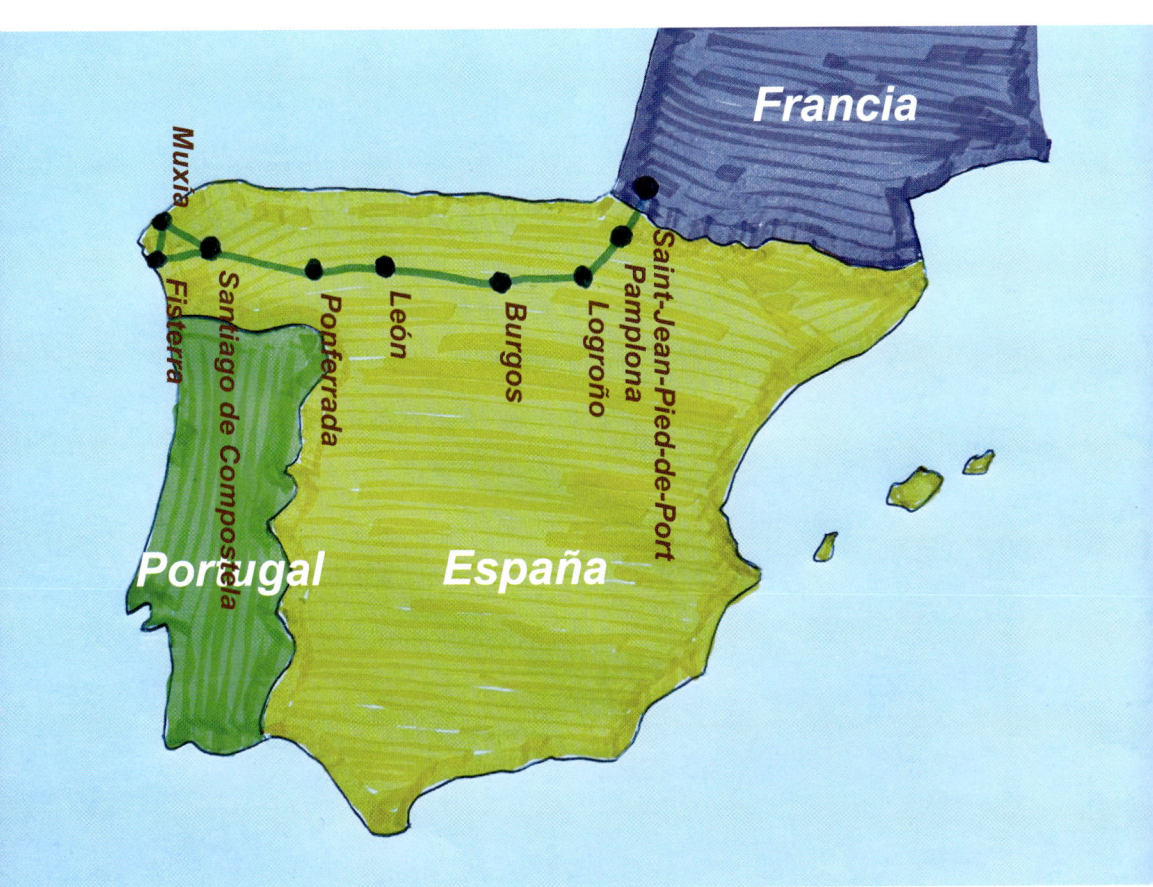

생장피에드포르
Saint-Jean-Pied-de-Port

796km

프랑스 순례길 출발점
설레는 마음과 두려운 마음이 교차하는
눈부시게 아름다운 마을

Starting point of the French Camino de Santiago
With excitement and a bit of fear
I walk into a most beautiful village

누구는 성당에서
누구는 강가에서
마음속으로 '부엔 카미노'를 외쳐 본다

In a cathedral
or by the river
In our minds, we are saying, 'Buen Camino!'

피레네산맥
Pyrénées Mts

변화무쌍한 날씨
무거운 배낭과 가파른 비탈길
숨은 턱에 차지만 멋진 풍경에 마음은 깃털 같다

Fickle weather
Heavy backpack, steep slope
I'm out of breath, but the view lightens my heart

피레네산맥을 넘기 전 마지막 프랑스 땅
여러 나라 사람들과 함께하는 설레는 밤이다

The French route's final stretch before the Pyrenees
A delightful night spent with people from all over the world

Orisson bar

Borda Alberge

반가운 푸드 트럭
프랑스 땅에서 맛보는 마지막 음식

The welcome sight of a food truck
This is the last meal before leaving France

스페인 땅으로 넘어가는 두 길이 있다
발카를로스와 나폴레옹 길
피레네산맥 정상을 넘는 나폴레옹 길은
순례길에서 가장 위험하고 아름다운 길이다
드디어 이 길에 들어섰다

There are two paths to the Spanish lands
The Valcarlos Route and the Napoleon Route
The Napoleon Route over the top of the Pyrenees
is the most strenuous and scenic trail
Finally, I am walking it

론세스바예스
Roncesvalles

771km

프랑스에서 스페인 땅으로
가장 힘든 피레네산맥을 넘었으니
절반은 성공이다

From France to Spain
I have crossed the hardest trail over the Pyrenees
It's a success already

부르게테
Burguete

768.0km

스페인 땅에서
처음 마주하는 아름다운 마을

The first village I come upon in Spain
is the beautiful Burguete

에스피날
Espinal

764.3km

어젯밤 내 아래 1층 침대의 아르헨티나 여성 순례자
우연이 인연으로 이어지는 반가운 만남
이색적인 풍경들이 배낭의 무게를 가볍게 해준다

A welcome sight of the pilgrim from Argentina
who used the bed below me the previous night
The exotic scenery eases the burden of my backpack

수비리
Zubiri

749km

걷는 내내 풀꽃 나무를 어루만지며
산새와 휘파람으로 화답하던
79세 프랑스 순례자

A 79-year-old pilgrim from France
caressed the grass, flowers, and trees as he walked
When he whistled to the birds, they whistled back to him

라라소아냐
Larrasoaña

743.5km

알베르게 신발장에 가지런히 놓인 신발들
마치 우리의 모습처럼 크기도 모습도 색깔도 제각각이다

Shoes neatly placed on racks in an albergue
All different in size, shape, and color, just like us

팜플로나
Pamplona

728.1km

순례자를 설레게 하는 첫 대도시
소몰이 축제로 유명한
과거와 현재가 조화를 이루는 곳

Known for its bullfighting festival
Pamplona is a big city with an imposing presence
Here, the past and the present co-exist in harmony

페르돈 고개
Alto del Perdón

716.3km

파란 하늘	Blue sky
하얀 구름	White clouds
초록 밀밭	Green fields of wheat
노란 유채꽃	Yellow canola flowers
순례자와 자전거	Pilgrims and bicycles

푸엔테 라 레이나
Puente la Reina

703.6km

오래된 성당
마을 끝에 자리한
우아한 '여왕의 다리'

There is an old cathedral
When I reach the end of the town
I see the elegant 'Bridge of the Queen'

시라우키
Cirauqui

695.9km

어린아이 세 명과 함께 걷고 있는 젊은 부부
무엇이 이들 가족을 길고 긴 순례길로 이끌었을까

A young married couple with three kids
I wonder what led them to this long and arduous road

에스테야
Estella

681.4km

강가의 아름다운 마을
밤새 걷고 싶은 곳

A splendid village by the river
I could walk here all night

이라체
Irache

677.4km

순례자 명소
수도원의 공짜 와인
전통을 이어 가는 대장간

A famous spot among pilgrims
There is free wine at the monastery
and a blacksmith shop carries on the traditional ways

수도원 지하 와이너리에 켜켜이 쌓여 있던
1933년산 와인은 어떤 맛일까

Lined up in the monastery's underground wine cellar are barrels of wine from 1933

비야마요르 데 몬하르딘
Villamayor de Monjardín

672.2km

언덕 정상에 성채가 남아 있는 마을
성당 담벼락에 기대앉아
알베르게 문 열리기를 기다리는 순례자

A small village with the remains of a citadel on top of the hill
Pilgrims are sitting outside the cathedral
waiting for the albergue to open

허허벌판에서 만난 반가운 푸드 트럭
공교롭게 모두 이탈리아 사람들이 모여
'아이 러브 유' 포즈로 기념사진을 찍는다

The timely appearance of a food truck
People, all from Italy, gather around for a photo
and make an 'I love you' sign with their hands

산솔
Sansol

652.6km

모처럼 이른 출발로 만난 해돋이
남들처럼 기념품을 살포시 걸어두고 소원을 빌어 본다

Starting early lets me catch the sunrise
I hang up a souvenir like those before me and make a wish

로그로뇨
Logroño

631.2km

순례길 두 번째 대도시
타파스 맛집만으로도 오래 기억될 곳
운 좋게 결혼식까지 덤으로 구경한다

Another big city on the Camino
The delicious tapas will not soon be forgotten
I even have the luck of watching a wedding ceremony

벤토사
Ventosa

612.7km

풍경이 아름다워 힘이 덜 드는 걸까
힘이 덜 들어 아름다운 걸까

The beautiful scenery makes me less tired
Perhaps being less tired makes everything more beautiful

나헤라
Nájera

601.7km

마을을 가로지르는 맑은 시냇물
언제나 갈증을 해소해 주던 시원한 맥주와 달콤한 오렌지주스
반대로 걷던 프랑스 순례자와 반갑게 눈인사를 나눈다

A clear stream flows across the town
Cold beer and sweet orange juice quench the thirst
I recognize a pilgrim from France, and we exchange smiles

시루에냐
Cirueña

587.4km

지는 해를 따라가다 만난 석양의 황금빛 밀밭
동틀 무렵에 마주하는 초록의 밀밭

As the sun is setting, I pass by a golden field of wheat
At dawn, I see a field of wheat, but this time it is green

그라뇽
Granón

573.1km

잠자리도, 같이 해 먹던 음식도
가장 기억에 남는 도네이션 알베르게

From the sleeping area to the meal we cooked and shared
this Donativo albergue stands out in my memory

벨로라도
Belorado

556.7km

꽃보다 아름다운 사람 모습
벽에 그려진 나 같은 모습

People in the field looking like flowers
The painting on the wall reminds me of myself

아헤스
Agés

528.7km

조용하고 한적한 작은 마을
마음 비우는 순례길에 일몰 일출 사진까지
자꾸 욕심이 늘어간다

A quiet and peaceful village
A pilgrim's mind is swayed by covetousness
as he reaches for images of the sunrise and sunset

아타푸에르카
Atapuerca

526.0km

최초의 유럽인으로 추정되는
유해가 발견된 마을

The oldest known European human fossil
was found in this village

푼토 데 비스타
Punto de Vistar

524.0km

고된 순간마다
곳곳에서 마주하는 십자가
다시 힘을 내게 한다

At every hard moment
the sight of the cross here and there
gives me the strength to go on

부르고스
Burgos

505.8km

순례길 세 번째 대도시
가는 날이 장날이라고, '백야 축제'
밤새 즐기다 노숙하던 날이다

The third big city I come upon on the Camino
By happenstance, the 'White Nights Festival' is going on
I spend the whole night outside, joining the fun

스페인 고딕 건축의 최고 걸작
부르고스 대성당

The Burgos Cathedral
A masterpiece of Spanish Gothic architecture

라베 데 라스 칼사다스
Rabé de las Calzadas

492.4km

벽화가 아름다운 마을
아인슈타인, 간디, 마틴 루터 킹, 그리고 순례자

A village with magnificent murals
Pilgrims stand next to Einstein, Gandhi, and Martin Luther King

오르니요스 델 카미노
Hornillos del Camino

484.5km

처음 시작되는 메세타를 거쳐 도착한 작고 예쁜 마을
마을을 서성이다 만난 옛 성터와 꽃 양귀비

Starting out on the Meseta, I come to a small, pretty village
There, I discover an old castle site and a poppy field

온타나스
Hontanas

473.7km

아름다운 마을과 성당
세계 각국의 성경 가운데 태극기가 선명한 한글 성경
'모두에게 평화, 2017 장 마리아'

A beautiful village and its cathedral
A Korean Bible catches my eye
'Peace for all, 2017, Maria Jang'

산 안톤
San Antón

467.9km

14세기 수도원 유적

보조 배터리를 빌려 주며 30분이나 기다려 준 독일인 천사

The ruins of a 14th-century monastery
An angle from Germany lends me a battery and waits while I take pictures

카스트로헤리스
Castrojeriz

464.1km

천사 덕분에 얻은 사진
끝없이 펼쳐진 아마폴라, 꽃 양귀비

This photo of a poppy-strewn field was taken
with the help of an angel

전쟁의 흔적이 남아 있는 역사적인 마을
한국인이 운영하는 알베르게에서 맛보는 비빔밥

A historic village with traces of war
At an albergue run by a Korean, pilgrims are served bibimbap

모스텔라레스 고개
Alto de Mostelares

460.1km

해발 600~900m 고원, 메세타
끝이 보이지 않는 밀밭과 아마폴라
꿈속을 거니는 듯 선경이다

The Meseta is a vast plateau with elevations of 600-900 meters
Endless fields of wheat and poppies
This is a fairyland seen in dreams

이테로 데 라 베가
Itero de la Vega

452.8km

끝없이 이어지는 밀밭
부자지간 부부지간의 정이 돈독해지는 길

Walking along the wheat fields
Family members can grow to love each other more

보아디야 델 카미노
Boadilla del Camino

444.4km

마을을 배회하다 마주친 안토니오 가우디가 연상되는 건축물
알베르게에서 즐기는 망중한

Wandering around, I come across an edifice reminiscent of Antonio Gaudi
I get to enjoy some time off at an albergue

카스티야 운하
Canal de Castilla

442.8km

18세기에 건설된 200km에 이르는 대운하
수로 따라 걷는 호젓한 길이다

This is a 200km long canal built in the 18th century
I walk through a quiet path along the waterway

비얄카사르 데 시르가
Villalcázar de Sirga

424.8km

7명의 알베르게 저녁식사 자리
프랑스 순례자가 식탁 종이에 여섯 명을 차례로 그리고
중국 순례자가 프랑스 순례자를 그려 7명의 그림이 완성되었다
각자 이름까지 적은 보물 같은 그림이다

Dinner at an albergue attended by seven pilgrims
A French pilgrim draws six of us on the paper tablecloth
A Chinese pilgrim draws in the French pilgrim
The drawing of all seven pilgrims is completed

카리온 데 로스 콘데스
Carrión de los Condes

418.8km

로마시대 이전부터 사람들이 살던 오래된 도시
성당, 수녀원, 수도원이 여럿 남아 있는 신앙적으로 의미 깊은 곳이다
순례길에서 여러 날을 마주치다 보니 이제는 모두 반가운 친구

An old town where people have lived since before the Romans
There are several churches, convents, and monasteries
Spending many days on the Camino, everyone becomes a friend

칼사디야 데 라 케사
Calzadilla de la Cueza

401.3km

작고 작은 아담한 마을
노을 구경하다 알베르게 문이 잠겨 노숙할 뻔했던 곳

A very small village
Lost in the sunset, I almost get locked out of the albergue

레디고스
Ledigos

394.8km

언제 봐도 부드러운 흙담
함께 즐기는 그림자놀이

A mud wall is always nice to look at
and an excellent background for a shadow play

모라티노스
Moratinos

388.3km

순례길 절반을 지나서일까
얼굴도 마음도 여유로워 보인다

Having passed the halfway point
there is an air of ease around us

사아군
Sahagún

378.2km

절반을 걸었다는 증명서를 만들어 주는 순례자 마을
오랜 역사가 묻어나는 산 만시오 경당
마을 끝에 자리한 아담한 칸토 다리

A town where you can get a halfway certificate issued
La Capilla de San Mancio emanates its long history
On the edge of the town lies the Puente Canto

베르시아노스 델 레알 카미노
Bercianos del Real Camino

368.1km

갈림길, 어디로 가야 하나
걷다 보니 흙집이 예쁜 마을길로 들어섰다

Standing at a crossroads, I wonder where I should go
I soon find myself in a village with lovely mud houses

엘 부르고 라네로
El Burgo Ranero

360.2km

마을의 수호성인 이름을 딴 성 베드로 성당
자원봉사자의 따스한 마음이 느껴지는 도네이션 알베르게

Iglesia de San Pedro, named after the village's patron saint
I meet a warm-hearted volunteer at the Donativo albergue

만시아 데 라스 물라스
Mansilla de las Mulas

340.8km

동틀 무렵 짙푸른 여명, 이제 익숙해진 새벽길의 순례자
걷다가 이른 시각에 문을 연 식당에서 아침 식사

The deep bluish light of early morning is no longer unfamiliar
Even at this hour, a tapas bar is open for breakfast

레온
León

321.7km

고대 왕국의 역사를 간직한 대도시
스페인 고딕 건축의 걸작, 산타 마리아 대성당

A modern city with a history of an ancient kingdom
The Santa Maria Cathedral, a remarkable monument
of Spanish Gothic art

산타 마리아 대성당의 우아하고 매혹적인 스테인드글라스

The enchanting stained glass windows
of the Santa Maria Cathedral

안토니오 가우디 건축물, 카사 보티네스
그리고 수년째 순례 중인 진정한 순례자

The Casa Bottines, a creation of Antonio Gaudi's
A pilgrim who has been on the trail for years

산 마르코스 광장 십자가 아래의 순례자상
알베르게 한 달 숙박비보다 비싼 파라도르 국영호텔
의외로 맥주와 커피는 안 비싸다

A statue of a pilgrim underneath the cross in the Plaza San Marcos
Hotel Parador, where a day's lodging costs
more than a month's at an albergue
Surprisingly, the hotel's beer and coffee are not expensive

발베르데 데 라 비르헨
Valverde de la Virgen

310.1km

갈림길이 나오면 으레 좁은 길로 향한다
그 길은 멀지만 예쁜 경치를 보여준다
오늘은 숙소를 예약해서 넓은 길을 택했는데
도로 따라 걷는 가장 지루한 길이었다
그래도 하늘의 구름은 예뻤다

산 마르틴 델 카미노
San Martín del Camino

296.2km

At a fork in the road, I usually go for the narrower path
The path may be long and winding, but beautiful
For once, I took the wider road to get to an accommodation
It was the most tedious path
But the clouds in the sky were still marvelous

푸엔테 데 오르비고
Puente de Órbigo

289.2km

순례길에서 가장 길고 오래된 다리
이 다리를 중심으로 두 마을로 나뉜다
중세 때부터 이어진 마상 창 시합,
지나는 길에 축제 준비가 한창이다

오스피탈 데 오르비고
Hospital de Órbigo

288.8km

The longest and oldest bridge on the Camino
The Hospital de Órbigo borders two villages
Preparations are on the way for a festival
where medieval jousting tournaments are recreated

지치고 허기질 무렵
신기루처럼 나타난 풍요로운 도네이션 먹거리
실컷 먹고 내고 싶은 만큼 내면 되는 곳

When exhaustion and hunger hits you
A donation food stand appears like a mirage
You can eat and pay as much as you want

아스트로가
Astorga

271.5km

위대한 안토니오 가우디의 건축물, 주교 궁전
스테인드글라스가 펼쳐내는 신비스러운 빛의 마술

The Palacio Episcopal, designed by the great Antonio Gaudi
The stained glass windows are magical works of art

무리아스 데 레치발도
Murias de Rechivaldo

266.7km

비다운 비를 만난 하루
그래도 모두 즐거운 표정이다

Despite rain pouring all day
everyone looks happy

산타 카탈리나 데 소모사
Santa Catalina de Somoza

262.1km

언제 비가 왔냐는 듯 파란 하늘과 하얀 구름
그리고 다음 행선지로 향하는 순례자의 발걸음

엘 간소
El Ganso

257.6km

The rain stops and the sky clears
On to the next destination

라바날 델 카미노
Rabanal del Camino

250.6km

한국인 신부님을 만날 수 있는 마을
그리고 세계 각국의 화폐가 붙어있는 알베르게
퇴계 이황이 일등, 무려 다섯 장이다

A village where you can find a Korean priest
On the wall of an albergue are bills of different currencies
Korea takes first place with five bills

폰세바돈
Foncebadón

245.0km

별 헤는 밤
모래알처럼 많은 별을 보며 걷다가
이른 새벽에 도착한 산골 마을

A starry night
Following the countless stars in the night sky
I reach a mountain village in the morning twilight

철십자가
Cruz de Ferro

244.2km

순례길 가장 높은 곳(1,504m)에 자리한 철십자가
저절로 기도하며 경건해지는 곳
밤새 동행한 폴란드 부부와 서로 감사 인사를 나눈다

The Iron Cross is located at the highest point on the Camino
I immediately bow and pray at the foot of the cross
I am thankful for the Polish couple who accompanied me all night

만하린
Manjarín

240.6km

순례길 가장 높은 곳에 위치한 알베르게
세계 각국의 도시까지 거리가 적혀 있는 문구,
로마 2,475km, 멕시코 9,636km
한국까지의 거리는 얼마나 될까

An albergue at the highest point on the Camino
There are signs with distances to places around the world
2,475km to Rome, 9,636km to Mexico
I wonder how far it is to Korea

엘 아세보
El Acebo

233.5km

기나긴 내리막길 끝에 만나는
1,100m 고도의 작은 산간 마을

After a long walk downhill
I reach a small village at an altitude of 1,100m

몰리나세카
Molinaseca

225.4km

굽이굽이 산길을 지나
하루쯤 쉬고 싶던 정감 어린 마을

A winding mountain path
led to a charming village

폰페라다
Ponferrada

217.5km

템플기사단 성채가 멋스러운 도시
맛난 음식 먹으며 며칠이고 쉬어 가고 싶은 곳

A city with the magnificent 'Castillo de los Templarios'
I could stay here for days enjoying good food and resting

노을 지는 성벽 아래
일몰 사진을 찍다가
나를 위해 연주해 주던 여인

Beneath the castle walls
a woman was taking pictures of the sunset
before she started playing music for me

비야프랑카 델 비에르소
Villafranca del Bierzo

193.4km

조용하고 평화로운 마을
성당과 수도원이 여럿 남아 있는 영성 가득한 곳이다
예능 프로그램 '스페인 하숙' 촬영지

A quiet and peaceful town
This is a spiritual place with many old churches and monasteries
The TV show 'Korean Hostel in Spain' was filmed here

베가 데 발카르세
Vega de Valcarce

176.2km

마을이 예뻐 머물렀던 알베르게
한글 안내문도 있다
열정적인 스페인과 브라질, 거기에 대만과 한국인 순례자
신바람 나는 저녁식사 자리였다

I stayed at this albergue because the village was so enchanting
There was a hand-written notice in Korean
Pilgrims from Spain, Brazil, Taiwan, and Korea
We had the best time at dinner

루이텔란
Ruitelán

174.0km

출발한 지 얼마 안 되었지만
그냥 지나칠 수 없는 예쁜 식당, '오메가'

Starting out the day
I come upon 'OMEGA', a pretty cafe that I cannot pass up

라스 에레리아스
Las Herrerías

172.6km

물레방아가 생각나는 개울가 예쁜 마을
지금부터는 급경사 오르막의 고행길이다

A lovely village by a stream that reminds me of a waterwheel
From here on, it is going to be a steep climb

라구나 데 카스티야
Laguna de Castilla

166.9km

고지대에 자리한 레온 지역 마지막 마을
지나온 여정이 고되게 느껴진다

The last village on the hills of León
The arduousness of the journey starts to sink in

갈리시아 표지석
Galicia Signstone

160.9km

순례길 마지막 오르막길에서 마주한 새로운 표지석
이제는 갈리시아 지방이다

On the last uphill walk on the Camino, a new sign stone appears
I am now entering the Galicia region

오 세브레이로
O Cebreiro

164.6km

갈리시아 지역의 첫 마을
'성체의 기적'으로 유명한 왕립 산타마리아 성당
그리고 힘든 하루를 보상하는 해넘이

The first village in Galicia
The Royal Santa Maria Cathedral, famous for 'Miracles of the Eucharist'
The view of the sunset makes up for a hard day

순례자가 모두 떠난 알베르게에서
혼자 본 경이로운 운해

After all the other pilgrims have left the albergue
I stay and watch a wonderous sea of clouds

산 로케 고개
Alto do San Roque

160.5km

1,270m 고개에 우뚝 서 있는 산 로케 순례자상
다른 순례자상들에 비해 위치도 규모도 느낌도 남다르다

A statue of a pilgrim on top of the 1,270m hill
It stands out in its location, size, and posture

오 비두에도
O Biduedo

149.9km

순례길 걷다 마주치는 수없이 많은 성당들
작고 아담한 성당에 더 정이 간다

There are numerous cathedrals one encounters on the Camino
I find the small ones to be more endearing

트리아카스텔라
Triacastela

143.2km

하루 종일 긴 내리막길을 걸어 도착한 마을
이런저런 생각이 드는 밤이다

After a long day's walk downhill, I finally arrive at a village
This is a night with a lot on my mind

사모스
Samos

132.6km

오랜 역사와 전통의 사모스 수도원
저절로 설명에 귀 기울이게 되는 성스러운 그림
정성스레 불 밝히는 촛불은 늘 마음을 평온하게 한다

The Samos monastery has a long history and tradition
I pay close attention to descriptions of the sacred paintings
Lighting a candle with care brings peace to the mind

사리아
Sarria

117.6km

예나 지금이나 순례길의 거점 도시
새로 출발하는 많은 순례자가 더해지는 곳이다
사리아 가는 길의 전원 풍경이 참 좋았다

Sarria has long been the central spot of the Camino
Many new pilgrims start their journey here
The scenery on the way to Sarria was very pleasant

루고
Lugo

웅장하고 성스러운 대성당,
신비롭고 아름다운 천장 그림과 스테인드글라스
일정을 착각해서 뜻하지 않게 다녀온 곳이다
이런 것이 여행의 참맛 아닐까

A majestic cathedral
with mystical paintings on the ceiling and stained glass windows
This was an unintended visit due to a mistaken itinerary
A serendipitous travel moment

오늘도 가는 날이 장날, 운 좋게 또 축제다
전통을 이어 가며 많은 사람들이 함께 즐기는 모습이 부럽기도 하다

Another local festival that I run into by pure luck
Seeing so many people gathered in celebration of tradition
makes me envious

로마시대의 성곽이 온전히 남아 있는 유일한 도시
옛 모습 그대로인 경이로운 성벽 길
순례길에서 가장 인상 깊은 장소였다

The only city where the ancient Roman walls remain intact
The long circuit of walls is a sight to behold
This is the most impressive place on the Camino for me

렌테
Rente

112.2km

안개 자욱한 신비로운 순례길
무거운 배낭에 나란히 손수레를 끌고 가는 순례자
풍경도 사람도 아름답다

A foggy and mystical trail
Two pilgrims walk side by side, pulling a cart together
The scenery and the people are both beautiful

아 페나
A Pena

100.0km

남은 거리 100.0km
너도나도 다양한 모습으로 기념사진
참 많이도 왔다

The remaining distance is 100.0km
Everyone is busy taking pictures to take back with them
It's hard to believe how far we've come

메르카도이로
Mercadoiro

99.3km

이틀 연속 몽환적인 아침
오늘도 짙은 안개로 꿈길을 걷는 듯
하얀 눈이 대지를 덮듯, 걷는 내내 세상이 깨끗하다

For two days in a row, the morning looks like a dream
Walking through a thick fog, I feel that I may be dreaming
The World is clean, as if covered in snow

포르토마린
Portomarín

94.4km

그냥 지나쳐 아쉬운 곳
마음속으로 멋진 모습을 그려 본다

This is a town I'm sorry to pass by
I draw up a wonderful image in my mind

리곤데
Ligonde

77.7km

중세에 왕들이 머물렀던 중요한 순례 마을
눈에 들어오는 문구에서 기념사진
'내가 곧 길이요 진리요 생명이니'

An important site for pilgrims where medieval kings used to stay
The phrase on the wall:
'I am the way, the truth, and the life.'

팔라스 데 레이
Palas de Rei

68.9km

12세기에 지어진 산 티르소 성당
중세 때부터 이어진 순례 도시답게 늘어난 순례자가 실감 난다
삼삼오오 복장도 배낭도 단출하다

The Iglesia de San Tirso was built in the 12th century
This is a town where pilgrims have been meeting since medieval times and it continues to draw pilgrims today

멜리데
Melide

54.0km

갈리시아 대표적인 문어 요리, '풀포(뽈뽀)'
초고추장에 찍어 먹는 문어가 더 그립다
이제 야경을 즐길 정도로 여유로워졌나 보다

Galicia's signature octopus dish, 'Pulpo'
But I miss octopus dipped in red pepper paste
I find myself relaxed enough to appreciate the night view

아르수아
Arzúa

39.4km

이제는 풍경보다 사람들의 모습에 더 눈길이 간다
3대가 같이 걷고 있는 미국의 대가족
홀로 숙소 고민하는 청년

I'm now more interested in people than the landscape
A large American family of three generations walking together
A young man looking for an albergue

공립 알베르게 문 열리기를 기다리는 순례자
노을 따라갔다 만난 천사 수녀님
모두가 그립고 그리운 추억이다

Pilgrims waiting for a public albergue to open
An angel of a nun I came to know while chasing the sunset
All are cherished memories

아스퀸타스
As Quintas

33.0km

누구는 자전거로, 누구는 걸어서
이제 산티아고까지 33km
기쁜 마음보다 아쉬운 마음 가득하다

On a bicycle or on foot
We're only 33km away from Santiago
I'm sad rather than happy that it's soon going to be over

몬테 도 고소
Monte do Gozo

4.8km

산티아고에서 가장 가까운 마을
순례길 마지막 밤이다
내일이면 눈물이 날지 모른다

The nearest village to Santiago
This is the last night of the pilgrimage
I might cry tomorrow

산티아고
Santiago de Compostela

0.0km

마침내 49일 만에 산티아고에 입성
눈물이 날 줄 알았는데 의외로 담담하다
산티아고 대성당에서 미사를 드리며 지나온 여정에 감사

I finally make it to Santiago in 49 days
I thought I was going to cry, but I'm surprisingly calm
During the pilgrim's mass at the cathedral,
I give thanks for the journey I've had

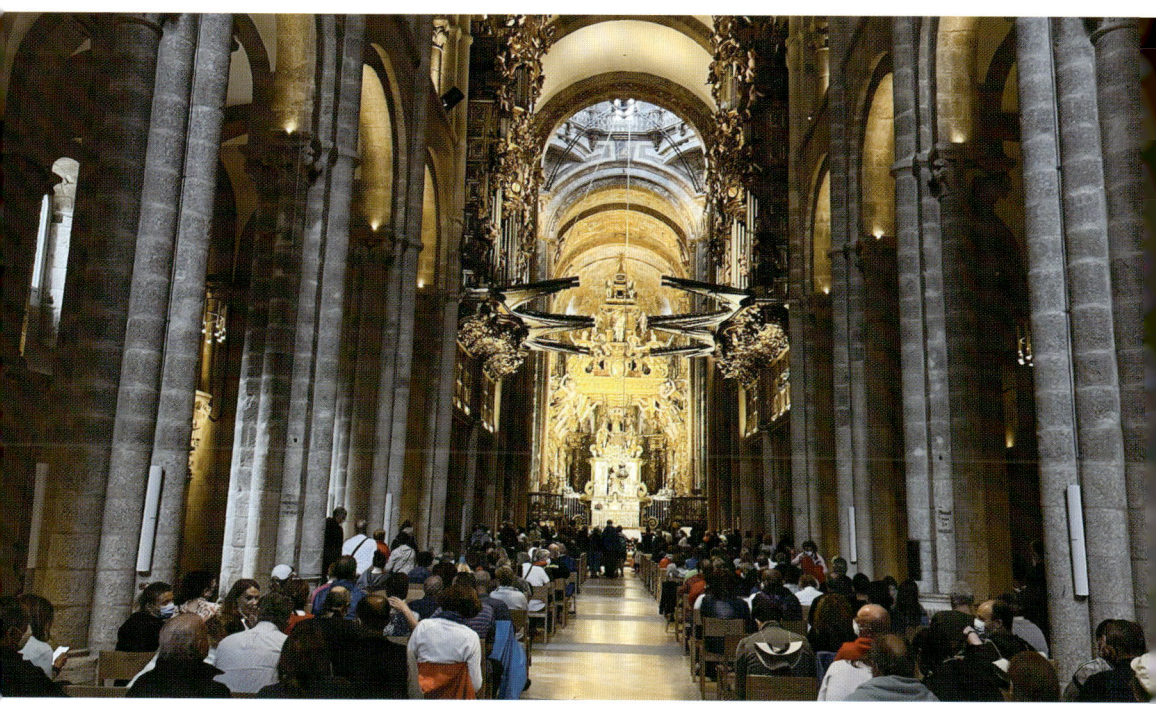

성당 광장의 순례자 모두 들뜨고 행복한 모습
서로 격려하고 축하 인사를 나눈다

The pilgrims in the cathedral square all look elated
We happily congratulate one another

광장의 순례자 모습도 각양각색이다
누구는 누워서 무념무상
누구는 가랑비 내리는 차가운 돌바닥에 엎드려 기도
그녀의 간절한 기도가 이루어지길 소망한다

The pilgrims in the square are engaged in diverse behaviors
Some lie on the ground free from all thought
Some kneel down and pray despite the drizzle
I wish her sincere prayers will be met

수고한 나를 위한 선물, 산티아고 파라도르
하루 방값이 지내온 알베르게 한 달치 비용보다 비싸다

As a gift to myself, I stay at the Santiago Parador
The room for one day there costs more than
for a month at an albergue

운이 따르던 순례길
내 방 창문으로 혼자 보는 풍광이다
이른 새벽과 늦은 밤에

I look back on my journey full of good luck
This is the view through the window that I have to myself
Early morning and late night

피스테라
Fisterra

0.00km

순례의 아쉬움이 남는 사람들이 더 가는 곳
유럽 대륙의 끝이자 대서양의 시작
0.00km 표지석과 고단함을 감내해 준 신발 표식
더는 순례자가 갈 수 없는 이곳이 바로, 땅끝이다

This is the place people go to because
they can't part with the Camino yet
The end of continental Europe
and the beginning of the Atlantic Ocean
The 0.00km sign stone and the shoe that endured it all
Where pilgrims can go no farther
This is the end of the earth

땅 끝까지 온 고단한 순례자를 맞이하는 순례자상
그리고 내게 허락된 아름다운 해넘이

A pilgrim's statue welcomes the weary pilgrim who has come to the end of the earth
And I am allowed one more beautiful sunset

피스테라 항구의 멋진 풍경과 해돋이
평생 살고 싶은 마을이다

Great scenery and sunrise at Fisterra harbor
This is a place I would like to live the rest of my life

가장 호사스러운 식당에서 가장 우아한 식사
여전히 알베르게 문 열리기 기다리는 긴 배낭 행렬
운명처럼 땅끝 마을에서 재회한 미국인 순례자

The most elegant meal in the most luxurious restaurant
A long queue of backpackers wait for the opening of an albergue
Amazingly, I am reunited with a pilgrim from the US

무시아
Muxía

0.00km

순례길 마지막 목적지
영화 '더 웨이'처럼 순례길 마침표로 점찍은 곳이다

As in the movie, 'The Way,' this place had been chosen
as the ending point of my pilgrimage

석조 기념물, 라 에리다
바다에서 가장 가까운 성당
마을이 내려다보이는 산 정상의 정감 어린 돌 십자가

A stone monument called La Herida
A cathedral close to the sea
A stone cross on top of a mountain overlooking the village

내일이면 순례자에서 일상의 여행자로 돌아간다
해안가의 호젓한 마을을 두 번이나 배회하며
조금은 영성이 깊어진 나 자신을 기대해 본다

Tomorrow, I will go from being a pilgrim to a daily traveler
Roaming twice through the quiet village on the coast
I wished that I may gain a little bit of spiritual growth

서울
Seoul

10,061.6km

사진 전시회

경치가 아름다운 순례길
그보다 더 빛나는 것은 사람과의 만남이다

Photo exhibition

A pilgrimage to beautiful sites
Meeting people has been even more beautiful

한 번도 가 보지 않은 사람은 있어도
한 번만 가 본 사람은 없다는 산티아고 순례길
다시 갈 그날을 기대해 본다

'부엔 카미노'

'Camino de Santiago'
They say there are those who haven't walked the Camino,
but no one has walked it just once
I look forward to the day I go back

'Buen Camino'

김창현 金昌鉉
Changhyun Kim

역사가, 사진가
Historian, Photographer
저서로 『누정 산책』 등이 있다.
여행, 답사, 사진을 좋아한다.

꿈꾸는 길, 산티아고
Dreaming Camino, Santiago

글·사진 김창현

초판 1쇄 발행일 2023년 5월 1일
발행인 이규상
편집인 안미숙
발행처 눈빛출판사
　　　서울시 마포구 월드컵북로 361 14층 105호
　　　전화 336-2167 팩스 324-8273
등록번호 제1-839호
등록일 1988년 11월 16일
편집 진행 Lee Dah
인쇄 예림인쇄
제책 일진제책
값 20,000원
copyright ⓒ 2023, 김창현
Published by Noonbit Publishing Co., Seoul, Korea
Printed in Korea

ISBN 978-89-7409-616-8 03660